What Our Readers Have Said...

"The Pinpoint Training Series delivers information that could be used in a lot different areas."

•

"Applicable and valid. The information is good."

•

"I like this because I can take them with me to read at a convenient time. I feel the little time I have to spend in the office is best use on activities that directly relate to revenue opportunities. I like the short amount of time it takes to keep up with these."

•

"I like the fact that the format allows the books to be reviewed as time permits. All work has been conducted on personal, evening/weekend time."

•

"My thought is that the real value of these books comes into effect when doing the action plans."

•

"The challenge when I think a specific topic does not apply is to find a way to make it apply."

•

"Short and sweet. These books are easy to comprehend."

•

"These books are very easy to read and clearly outlined."

•

"I have enjoyed reading these books. They are relevant to today's work environment and the ongoing change in the way we manage our workforce."

•

"I believe the contents of the Pinpoint series are excellent. It causes one to reflect on the daily dynamics in working with oneself as well as with management and peers."

•

"Most of the information in these would help an open-minded management person, or an inexperienced management person."

•

"These books will pay for the time that I am investing. There are numerous good ideas that will streamline what I do and how I do it."

•

"All and all I think the Pinpoint series is a good program. I know other people I would love to have something like this. I think a lot of the suggestions are very useful, and can be applicable to everyday situations. If nothing else it's a good reference guide to fall back upon if a situation arises in the future."

•

"These books reinforce many concepts that I have learned through seminars, schooling and other programs. For myself, it serves as a constant learning tool that keeps me on top of the issues that many of us encounter every day."

•

"All in all, I think you have good training books. It helps everyone to review these materials, it serves as a good reminder to us on how to conduct ourselves."

•

"The information is valuable in these books."

•

Professional Development

Pinpoint Sales Management Skill Development Training Series

TIMOTHY F. BEDNARZ

MAJORIUM
BUSINESS PRESS

Pinpoint Sales Management Skill Development Training Series
"Professional Development"
Timothy F. Bednarz

Graphic design: Monika Pawlak

Majorium Business Press
2025 Main Street
Stevens Point, WI 54481
715.342.1018 • 800.654.4935

ISBN 978-1-62101-057-9

Printed in the United States of America

Introduction

The Pinpoint Sales Management Skill Development Training Series is designed for targeted training and education regarding increased improvement in a specific skill or competency.

Each book within this series is designed to be easy to use, understand and apply to your job. It can be used as a basis for training individuals, as a discussion guide or as a personal training tool.

Each chapter within this book discusses a specific concept. When you have completed all eight chapters you should have a 360º perspective of the topic.

Additionally, each chapter is divided into specific sections:

- The first section provides you with an overview of the topic
- The Implications section discusses why the concept is important, and why it is important to learn and apply.
- The Strategies, Tips & Techniques to Apply section teaches how to use and apply the particular concept to your work.
- The Points to Ponder section gives you something to think about or to be discussed with a group setting. These are questions not meant to be immediately answered, but to be pondered over time.
- The Training Activity section provides you with the tools to transfer what you have learned to your job. It is designed to help create an action plan to effectively apply the concept.

Each of the topics in this series is time-tested and proven in the marketplace. They have been used by thousands of employees as training tools. Many of the users have commented that what made these books valuable, was the ability to refer to them when a problem surfaced. They indicated that they remembered reading about the exact problem. They referred back to these books and found an appropriate solution.

You will find them equally valuable as a resource in your professional development library.

Table of Contents

1. The Need for Professional Development........ 1

2. Critical Skills that Determine Positive Self-Development........ 5

3. Becoming a Leader of Your Own Making........ 9

4. Overcoming Professional Development Hurdles........ 13

5. Taking the Right Action Steps........ 17

6. Maintaining Focus........ 23

7. Creative Decision Making........ 27

8. Factors Affecting Paradigm Thinking........ 31

LEARNING OBJECTIVES:

- To understand and apply the elements and factors of professional development.
- To identify the critical factors and benefits of professional development and the impact they have on the professional sales management growth process.
- To understand the implications and ramifications that enhance or diminish professional growth and the professional development process.
- To identify and overcome the problems and pitfalls associated with the professional development process.
- To apply effective strategies to enhance individual professional development.
- To understand cause and effect relationships and their impact as a result of failing to grow professionally.
- To identify how professional sales management development impacts the decision making process.
- To analyze the expected results and outcomes of professional sales management development.
- To apply alternative strategies to effectively enhance professional sales management growth and utilizing skills and strategies to increase levels of management awareness and effectiveness.

1

The Need for Professional Development

The events of the first years of the twenty first century caught many sales managers off guard and exposed a deficiency in their skills to be successful in the future. If anything, these events made many sales managers understand the need to change. Yet many are still unaware of the skills they will require to be successful going forward.

IMPLICATIONS — WHAT THIS MEANS TO YOU

Many sales managers wonder how they can develop their professional skills when they must also deal with the problems and daily crises that sap much of their time and energy. What's more, these pressures show no signs of easing, but instead will intensify in the future. Many sales managers feel completely overwhelmed by circumstances and events and at risk for more adverse ramifications in a results-oriented business environment.

It is important for sales managers to understand that their roadmap for future professional development provides them with the specific skill set they need to take control and manage the events that have besieged them. Unfortunately, such development requires a change in thinking and attitude that many feel unable to make, and this ultimately will cause their downfall.

STRATEGIES, TIPS & TECHNIQUES TO APPLY

Whether the individual sales manager likes it or not, whether economic conditions are booming or extremely stagnant, he or she is often leading in times of volatility and uncertainty. With this constant in mind, sales managers must follow a roadmap that provides them with the opportunity to professionally develop their personal skills and abilities. Some of the milestones of this roadmap include:

Embracing Change

Change is the greatest ongoing obstacle facing any sales manager. Its pace is ever-increasing, fueled by technological advances and increased global competition. No company or sales manager can resist change and stand still without being overtaken by events, circumstances and competition. Many find it easy to be resistant to change, hanging on to the status quo and relying on outmoded business models based on historical data. Yet what has worked in the past may not work in the future. Only when events and circumstances overrun management do many feel forced to change. However, being reactive rather than proactive leads to additional problems and repercussions that sales managers are forced to deal with.

The sales manager who wishes to grow professionally must first and foremost embrace change and its forces. By embracing change, sales managers can use it to drive their company forward. The idea is to channel any resistant energy instead into using change to push the organization toward taking advantage of the opportunities held by times of turmoil.

When sales managers embrace change, they are shifting their own thinking to a more proactive management stance. They then can harness the powers of change by anticipating its impact on the business and how best to take advantage of the resulting events and circumstances.

Facing Reality

With the ever-changing business environment comes alterations in reality that every business and sales manager must adapt to. The sales manager who avoids reality has his or her course set for failure. Only when sales managers face the situation head on and adapt their business and sales strategies to actual conditions can they hope to survive in the future. Undoubtedly, this is difficult for many sales managers who have carefully crafted plans and strategies around a business reality that no longer exists; however, it is an essential step if they are to develop professionally.

Leading with Vision

As sales managers personally develop their skills, business conditions demand that they act less like sales managers who merely control and direct and assume a more flexible leadership role allowing them to be increasingly responsive and adaptive to the changing business environment. This process shifts their thinking and attitudes and gives them both the openness and flexibility to lead in volatile and uncertain times. It is the sales manager as leader's vision of the future that is the guiding force for the organization; they must continually communicate their personal vision with passion at every available opportunity.

Setting General, Flexible Goals

Sales managers no longer have the luxury to micromanage their salespeople and organization with plans, goals and objectives that anticipate every contingency. Rather, sales managers must set general and flexible goals that guide and direct their sales team, but do not restrict the freedom of action to respond to specific and unanticipated events, especially as businesses increasingly encounter uncontrollable circumstances. Sales managers must build flexibility into their plans for adjusting to such circumstances without adversely affecting the forward progress of the overall organization.

Focusing on What's Working

As sales managers personally adapt to the forces of change, they must maintain the ability to both recognize and expand upon what is working in the current environment. Outdated and outmoded practices hindering performance must be quickly eliminated. As what works one day might not be effective the next day, sales managers must be open to changing business methods and practices that achieve the overall goals and objectives of the organization.

POINTS TO PONDER — SOMETHING TO THINK ABOUT

1. Do you feel you are being controlled by events and circumstances, or that you control them?
2. How well have you adapted to the environment and events of the past two years?

TRAINING ACTIVITY — APPLICATION & ACTION PLAN

Conduct a personal audit of your professional skills.

1. On a sheet of paper list the following factors.
    - Embracing Change
    - Facing Reality
    - Leading with Vision
    - Setting General, Flexible Goals
    - Focusing on What's Working
2. Contrast your current actions and thinking with what will be required of you in the future.
3. Determine what actions you need to take to achieve any future milestones.

2

Critical Skills that Determine Positive Self-Development

The complexion of management is changing. The skills required of sales managers in the past have become outdated and outmoded by the volatile business environment. Sales managers are required to adapt or lose their professional effectiveness. There are a number of critical skills they must master if they are to remain relevant in their company.

IMPLICATIONS — WHAT THIS MEANS TO YOU

Most sales managers would like to maintain the status quo. It is easy to be resistant to change and its impact on the business environment. In fact, many sales managers are doing just that, hoping that conditions will revert to the way they were in the past. Unfortunately, this wishful thinking has numerous adverse consequences.

It is important for sales managers to understand and grasp that things will never be the same and that the impact of change is a reality they must comprehend and deal with. This demands an ongoing adjustment in thinking and attitude that must continually evolve with shifts in the global marketplace. New skills are required of sales managers to integrate these changes into their business.

STRATEGIES, TIPS & TECHNIQUES TO APPLY

Sales managers must understand that there are a number of skills they must develop that constitute enhanced self-improvement and professional development. None of these skills are independent of the sales manager's job performance. They must have the professional ability to:

Think Outside the Box

Most sales managers' thinking is shaped by the events and circumstances that they have experienced. Over time an individual's perception has the tendency to become myopic—completely focused on the activities of the company and its internal units. Therefore, the sales manager's thought process includes a bias that may not reflect reality.

Change and its related forces demand that sales managers climb outside of their points of reference to develop a fresh perspective of their company and the realities of the business environment. This action often results in a paradigm shift that impacts future business practices and methods. Sales managers are compelled to recognize the dynamic reality of the general environment and how change is impacting their business.

Change the Culture

Linked with the paradigm shift is the required alteration in the corporate culture that is necessitated by change. Sales managers often have difficulty dealing with the concept of changing the culture around them, mostly out of fear of the personal consequences that come with challenging conventional wisdom. What most sales managers fail to understand is that they must evolve as leaders, rather than as sales managers who merely supervise, and realize the subsequent risk they place themselves in by not assuming the leadership role that necessitates the change of culture. While complacent sales managers might keep the peace for the time being, the consequences of their failure to adapt will often catch up with them in the future.

Monitor Pulse of the Workplace

The professional development of sales managers demands that they delegate more tactical unit activities and responsibilities to their salespeople. While this pushes decision making down to the front lines where it has the most impact, it does not mean the sales manager should ignore what is happening with his or her workforce. Rather, they should use performance metrics to keep a daily pulse on what is actually happening on the floor. While they should delegate their micromanagement activities, it is important to maintain an active presence with their salespeople. This allows them to proactively interact with any individual when needed.

Act Quickly

As sales managers create a leadership style, they also must incorporate the ability to act quickly and decisively. In a business environment of rapid change, hesitancy is not a desirable trait, especially when a failure to act can easily open up an opportunity for the competition.

Keep It Simple

While many sales managers have developed the notion that a complicated plan or goal is sophisticated, the successful sales manager understands the need to keep things simple and to stress execution.

Complicated plans and solutions demand complicated and costly support systems. Such plans are also highly prone to human error, which further increases the risk of failure. Conversely, simple plans and goals are less expensive, are not as prone to error, and are more easily executed.

Develop Self-Confidence

Sales managers who desire to professionally develop their sales managerial skills must cultivate a sense of confidence in their own decisions. Many fall into the trap of always second-guessing themselves, which results in hesitancy and loss of self-confidence in their abilities. Rather than hesitate, it is a more desirable sales managerial trait to act quickly and decisively and then, if necessary, correct the decision later as additional data and results become available.

POINTS TO PONDER — SOMETHING TO THINK ABOUT

1. How proactive are you in developing necessary leadership skills?
2. What prevents you from developing newly required skills?

TRAINING ACTIVITY — APPLICATION & ACTION PLAN

1. List the following skills on a sheet of paper. Identify which ones you are proficient in.
    - Thinking outside the box
    - Changing the culture
    - Monitoring the pulse of the workplace
    - Acting quickly
    - Keeping it simple
    - Developing self-confidence
2. Pinpoint particular areas of weakness that require improvement.
3. Based upon your self-assessment, create a program to strengthen certain necessary skills.

3

Becoming a Leader of Your Own Making

Whether the economy is robust or sluggish, market conditions are perilous and uncertain. Whole industries expand at dynamic rates of growth, while others collapse with similar intensity. Periods of volatility and uncertainty often represent an opportunity for leaders who dare to define themselves and take risks.

IMPLICATIONS — WHAT THIS MEANS TO YOU

There was a time when most sales managers had a well-defined professional life: their roles were established and responsibilities clearly delineated. Those times have ended, replaced by an era of change and upheaval. The relative tranquility experienced by sales managers in the past has been replaced by today's stress and turmoil.

It is important for sales managers to understand that the direct control roles of management are quickly being replaced by dynamics of leadership that include empowerment, trust and performance. It is no longer sufficient to simply direct and control; sales managers must become leaders capable of harnessing the dynamics of change. Change demands a leader who can passionately communicate a personal vision of what adaptation and flexibility can accomplish. Sales managers who are incapable of adapting to this leadership role will be quickly swept away.

STRATEGIES, TIPS & TECHNIQUES TO APPLY

The role of professional development takes on added significance in dynamic times. In the past, professional growth meant that a sales manager was adding, enhancing and polishing existing skills for future opportunities. Today, professional development requires complete transformation in the following areas:

Leading

While sales managers of the past simply directed, today's sales manager leads by becoming proactive in both their thinking and actions, taking challenges head on and searching for new opportunities and methods. This is opposed to the traditional sales manager's role of reacting to events as they occurred, and depending upon the circumstances, taking advantage of only obvious opportunities. Leaders don't have this luxury in the current environment: they must search out and find opportunities—and take advantage of them before the competition does.

Learning

Sales managers who lead develop a passion for learning while creating a similar environment within their organization. The dynamics of change create the demand for more knowledge and expertise. The traditional training model of one or two seminars a year is no longer applicable. Leaders must continually learn by constantly looking for new ideas, insights and concepts that they can translate and apply to their business environment.

Monitoring the Pulse of the Business

The principles of leadership include delegation, trust and communication. The application of these principles demands delegation of many traditional daily management tasks and decisions to frontline salespeople. As a result, many time-consuming tasks are removed from the sales manager's plate, but as a leader he or she must actively keep a finger on the pulse of their unit or department. The use of various reporting mechanisms enables sales managers to know what is going on at any moment, with deviations from predetermined measurement standards raising red flags signaling the need for intervention.

Focusing on the Long-Term

Sales managers as leaders are more strategic than tactical in their thinking. They learn to delegate or eliminate time-wasting tasks so that they are more available to accomplish their mission. With these tactical responsibilities removed, sales managers are able to develop the strategic thinking to move the organization forward. The time is then available for them to think outside the box to find new and innovative ways of increasing performance and results.

Taking Risks

Active leadership demands that sales managers take the risks needed to move their organization forward. It should be noted that chances are not taken impulsively without fully considering the consequences of undesirable outcomes. However, leaders do act quickly without hesitancy based upon their personal assessment and conviction.

Watching the Numbers

Effective leaders maintain a close eye on their financial statements, actively monitoring them for waste or excessive spending. They develop realistic budgets and hold closely to them throughout the year, making modifications where required. When possible, they link their performance metrics directly to their budgets to provide them with a more accurate picture of what is happening on a daily basis in their business.

POINTS TO PONDER — SOMETHING TO THINK ABOUT

1. Do you see yourself as a dynamic leader, a laid-back sales manager or somewhere in between?
2. Do you see more of a need to be a leader than a sales manager in the current business environment?

TRAINING ACTIVITY — APPLICATION & ACTION PLAN

Determine how well you are progressing in your professional development. Assess your performance development in each of the areas listed below. Develop a personal plan to eliminate any deficiencies.

- Leading
- Learning
- Monitoring the Pulse of the Business
- Focusing on the Long-Term
- Taking Risks
- Watching the Numbers

4

Overcoming Professional Development Hurdles

It is one thing to learn what a sales manager needs to do to professionally develop in order to adapt to the changes in the marketplace—and another to actually do it. Time and the pressures of the job make any development seemingly impossible; but it is possible when approached in the proper light.

IMPLICATIONS – WHAT THIS MEANS TO YOU

Whether a sales manager is formally trained or undertakes professional development on his or her own, there is a single purpose in mind: to change personal behavior in a way that produces positive results. While some behavioral change can be spontaneous, most happens incrementally over time.

It is important for sales managers to grasp that although they may feel compelled to change their behaviors quickly and dramatically, this often only results in additional stress and pressure on an already demanding job. Sales managers who are able to effectively change their behavior understand that adaptation occurs over time, and that by applying what they have learned in small doses they can gradually progress and achieve their desired results without undue stress and pressure.

STRATEGIES, TIPS & TECHNIQUES TO APPLY

The psychological nature of many sales managers induces them to be competitive. Their personality type compels them to take on a task, overcome it and move on. However, this approach to professional development will often result in failure and frustration due to the following factors:

Time

Time is the biggest hindrance to change and professional development. Sales managers are inundated with so many tasks and responsibilities that any initiative toward professional development is quickly forgotten as more pressing problems demand their time.

This strong demand for time is why an incremental approach to learning and development is far more effective. It may take longer than expected, but it will eventually happen rather than be forgotten or brushed aside. Sales managers who commit themselves to learning and applying one idea or concept a day—or one per week for that matter—will achieve their goals with persistence. This approach will also avoid any additional undue stress that may overwhelm the sales manager with the pressing need to learn and change immediately.

Focus

The demands of the average sales manager result in a loss of personal focus on the long-term professional development goals that are required for them to grow and develop as a leader.

Sales managers must understand the need to focus on these important developmental goals and not sacrifice them in the face of expediency. Once again, the incremental approach of breaking development goals into small steps allows sales managers to perform their tasks without sacrificing their professional development.

Daily Problems

The compelling pressures of daily problems and crises can easily distract sales managers not only from their professional development, but also from the accomplishment of their current goals and objectives. While it is difficult to get away from the demands of the customer, sales managers must devote a small portion of their day or week to taking small steps toward enhancing their professional ability. The key is to be persistent in both scheduling and investment of time.

Change

The dynamics of change are becoming a more pressing issue in every business. When thrown into the mix with the pressures of time, personal focus, daily problems, competition and salesperson performance, the world can appear filled with a number of spinning tops careening uncontrollably around and into each other. However, it is the existence of all of these forces that makes professional development and the transformation of the sales manager into a leader more important. It is only with the development of these skills that the sales manager will be able to make sense of his or her tumultuous environment. Rather than push aside the development of professional skills, the forces of change should make the average sales manager embrace the need to learn.

Competition

Increased competitive pressures puts another barrier in the way of sales manager development. Such issues shift a sales manager's focus to the immediate matters at hand and not to the time required to develop their professional skills. Yet the existence of a learning environment where sales managers can incrementally learn and apply new ideas, concepts and insights provides them with exactly the tools needed to deal with competitive pressures. When sales managers give themselves the opportunity to learn and enhance their skills, they are enabling themselves to get outside the box, if even for an instant. This opportunity can often provide them with insightful solutions to many competitive problems.

Performance and Motivation

In many aspects of business, the bottom line is performance, which is the reason sales managers exist. Their primary role is to ensure that individual salespeople are performing and producing at all times; this is the biggest and most time-consuming challenge facing sales managers.

It is a universally recognized fact that professional development has a significant bearing on performance. One of the goals of professional development is to make sales managers more effective leaders. As competent leaders, they have the tools to more effectively impact the performance of their team.

POINTS TO PONDER – SOMETHING TO THINK ABOUT

1. What are the biggest challenges you have faced in creating a successful professional development program for yourself?
2. How have you overcome these challenges?

TRAINING ACTIVITY – APPLICATION & ACTION PLAN

Below are listed the biggest barriers to change and professional development facing sales managers. Identify the specific strategies that you can use to overcome these barriers and create a channel for your own professional development.

- Time
- Focus
- Daily Problems
- Change
- Competition
- Performance and Motivation

5

Taking the Right Action Steps

In the face of overwhelming change, it is often difficult to predict the future with any certainty. Sales managers must have the flexibility to adapt to change and harness its forces to their advantage. In many cases the results of such an upheaval cause a shift in both thinking and actions. While this process can be difficult for some sales managers to adjust to, one thing is certain: they can either adapt or be bypassed. Market and business conditions are unforgiving to the sales manager who resists change.

IMPLICATIONS — WHAT THIS MEANS TO YOU

Sales managers must recognize that many of the traditional business models of the past are no longer applicable. A number of organizations have employed a host of management fads over the past decade with either limited success or disastrous results. Aside from the implementation of new ideas and concepts meant to enrich the authors rather than the company, it is certain that sales managers must deal with the ever-increasing forces of change that appear to be both overwhelming and unrelenting.

It is important for sales managers to understand that they are forced to adapt to and align themselves with the changes impacting their industry and company. The traditional direct-and-control role is being replaced by the principles of active leadership and empowerment as the most effective method to anticipate and handle changes in the business environment and marketplace. As a result, the sales manager is required to take a proactive rather than a passive stance. In this way leaders are on the alert and prepared to deal with the constantly changing business environment.

STRATEGIES, TIPS & TECHNIQUES TO APPLY

Sales managers must adapt to meet the demands of their company, customers and the marketplace. Their professional development and transformation into a proactive leader is interlinked with the changes their organization must make to survive and prosper. The shift can be accomplished by the continual application of the ideas listed below. Since change is continuous and relentless, the evolution of new ideas and professional development must also be ongoing.

Brainstorm

Sales managers must always be seeking new ideas to implement in their business. The best source of new ideas and insights lies within the native knowledge of their individual salespeople. They are positioned in the front lines of the business where they gather feedback from both coworkers and customers, and see firsthand what the competition is doing in the marketplace. Unfortunately, in many organizations this wealth of knowledge is seldom tapped, much less converted into a useful form. Yet this source of information, insight and ideas are at the sales manager's fingertips.

Sales managers need to schedule ongoing brainstorming sessions to utilize their salespeople's knowledge and work through ideas and concepts. Where geographically dispersed branches or locations prohibit this, sales managers should consider a threaded discussion group using email as a tool to engage their salespeople as a group.

Brainstorming has distinct advantages in that it feeds on participant synergy in order to build on ideas and concepts. Most participants feel energized and motivated when the exercise is properly undertaken and all ideas and feedback are considered and treated with respect.

Abandon Prejudices

Most seasoned sales managers have personal prejudices regarding how things in their business should be run. Formed from their experiences and successes over the span of their career, these biases can hinder a sales manager's ability to develop and implement new ideas and concepts. With the speed and impact of change in the world now, it is essential to know that what has worked in the past may no longer be effective, and that the fact that old processes may still be in place does not mean there are not better ways of doing things.

New ideas and concepts developed during brainstorming or from other forms of feedback should not be summarily dismissed as a "bad fit" for the corporate culture. Sales managers need to put aside their personal prejudices and examine viable ideas from all angles in order to determine whether they have an application or can improve salesperson and company performance.

Implement New Ideas

While sales managers should seek out new ideas from their salespeople, customers and their own research, more must be done. After developing these ideas, determining their applicability to the company, and prioritizing them, sales managers must then implement those that can have the most impact.

People generally fear that new approaches will not work. However, sales managers must overcome their reluctance by continually testing new ideas. If they do fail, they should learn from the experience and move on to other concepts. It is from a series of failures and the subsequent lessons learned that new and viable ideas are built.

Remove Barriers

Sales managers must remove barriers their salespeople may encounter that hinder their effectiveness, productivity and efficiency. In the sales environment, this can typically include reports as well as reworking procedures that hinder their ability to directly deal with a prospect or customer.

Sales managers need to measure what is actually needed versus what is currently required. The implementation of new ideas and the increase in the level of customer service may require a streamlining of procedures to enhance the individual salesperson's ability to be productive and attain desired results.

Think Small

From the mid-90s to the mid-00s there was a tendency for companies with a "bigger is better" mindset to expand through acquisitions and mergers. However, sales managers must now think small. This adjustment may include reorganizing units into smaller cells that are more adaptable to change. Additionally, thinking small should translate into the areas of goals and planning. IBM built their business on the philosophy of small successes. By breaking their goals down into a series of less daunting, more easily attained steps, salespeople were able to build their confidence and motivation by completing one after another. The outcome was the same as giving salespeople the entire goal at once, but in this manner it did not seem insurmountable.

Lead with Passion

As sales managers transform themselves into proactive leaders they must evolve in their style so that they lead with a passion, sharing their personal vision at every opportunity with their salespeople, customers and suppliers. They will find that their passion is contagious and that it will impact the performance of the entire team.

POINTS TO PONDER — SOMETHING TO THINK ABOUT

1. Have you aligned your personal thinking with the changes occurring within your organization, or are you resistant to new ideas?
2. How passionate are you about leading your team and implementing new ideas and concepts?

TRAINING ACTIVITY – APPLICATION & ACTION PLAN

1. Examine the following key concepts discussed in this chapter:
    - Brainstorm
    - Abandon Prejudices
    - Implement New Ideas
    - Remove Barriers
    - Think Small
    - Lead with Passion
2. Identify how many of these ideas you are currently applying.
3. Determine the depth of their application.
4. Determine any deficiencies in their application.
5. Create a plan to better implement and/or use additional concepts.

6

Maintaining Focus

While it is easy for sales managers to start out with the best of intentions, many can be detoured by the uncontrollable events impacting their professional lives and company. When a crisis occurs, there is a tendency to immediately confront the challenge. While well-intentioned and often necessary, sales managers should not allow this thinking to cause them to lose focus on their goals and development.

IMPLICATIONS – WHAT THIS MEANS TO YOU

Maintaining a results-oriented focus takes discipline and perseverance in the face of constant interruptions that demand both the sales manager's time and attention. If sales managers are focused in their thinking, it must be strategic in nature, concentrating on the long-term growth of the business rather than on the problem or crisis demanding their immediate attention. The ultimate solution to every problem must fit into the long-term goals of the sales manager.

It is important for sales managers to grasp that maintaining a focus on long-term goals and objectives and attaining a desired outcome is the result of doing the right things, at the right time, and in the right sequence. Often sales managers allow uncontrollable events and problems to make them lose sight of or even abandon their long-term plan and goals.

STRATEGIES, TIPS & TECHNIQUES TO APPLY

Sales managers who want to successfully maintain a results-oriented focus that allows them to consistently achieve their goals and desired outcomes must:

Develop Mental Discipline

Successful sales managers have developed the mental discipline that keeps them focused on their goals regardless of the problems and uncontrollable events they may encounter. Such hurdles must be overcome on the path to the successful accomplishment of their objectives.

Mental discipline allows sales managers to always keep an eye on their goals. They consistently keep the summit of the mountain in view, and do not allow daily problems to impede their progress. While daily problems may cause a setback, sales managers always make sure they are moving forward one step at a time.

Sales managers should understand that the attainment of mental discipline takes a conscious effort and perseverance. While not an easy road, it is achievable.

Adopt Strategic Thinking

To achieve and maintain a results-oriented focus, sales managers must learn to take a protracted view of their business, which means acquiring and polishing strategic thinking skills. These skills allow sales managers to create their focus and form part of their personal vision—the top of the mountain—in the first place.

The long view is opposed to tactical thinking that focuses only on short-term day-to-day activities. As companies evolve, many are empowering their salespeople and delegating the tactical activities lower in the organization. Salespeople assume much of the day-to-day decision making that directly impacts their performance and relationships with customers.

Plan

While strategic thinking was considered passé and outmoded during the heyday of the dot-coms, it is now clear that a lack of planning contributed mightily to their downfall. Successful sales managers develop a realistic plan, work the plan and stick to it. It is a simple concept, yet does require discipline.

A great deal of a plan's success lies in its execution. Many sales managers develop excellent plans, but, because they have not properly executed and held to them, fail to see their fruits. The best plans are not complex instruments, but simple and designed to be easily and effectively carried out.

Question Activities

Many sales managers have a natural tendency to want to control everything within their sphere of influence. Yet it is this desire that causes many to lose focus on their long-range plan as they attempt to personally put out every fire and handle every issue.

As leaders, sales managers must empower their salespeople and delegate the tasks, assignments and responsibilities that do not advance them toward the attainment of their desired outcomes. In this light, every activity on their to-do list and calendar must be questioned on a consistent basis; if a particular pursuit does not advance the sales manager toward the accomplishment of their goals, it should either be delegated or eliminated.

Monitor Results

Successful sales managers tie the metrics that measure their unit's progress directly to their plans. They then determine the frequency and content of the report that allows them to actively monitor progress toward their own and the organization's goals.

Additionally, sales managers have flags built into their metrics that immediately signal potential problems when the numbers reported to them are outside normal ranges. The report allows them to quickly act and resolve the problem before it gets out of hand.

POINTS TO PONDER – SOMETHING TO THINK ABOUT

1. Have you developed the mental discipline to maintain a results-oriented focus?
2. Are you easily taken off-focus by daily problems and crises that arise?

TRAINING ACTIVITY – APPLICATION & ACTION PLAN

The following activities and characteristics do not come automatically; it takes time, patience and discipline to develop and hone them into applicable skills.

- Develop Mental Discipline
- Adopt Strategic Thinking
- Plan
- Question Activities
- Monitor Results

1. Analyze your proficiency in each skill area in order to uncover any weaknesses.
2. Develop a personal plan for each of the areas including an improvement plan for any skills you feel you already have.
3. Implement your plan and monitor the results.

7

Creative Decision Making

The recessionary cycle of the early 2000s and events of September 11, 2001, underscore the turbulent times all businesses are currently experiencing. However, the times of the greatest business opportunity are times when the business environment is experiencing the greatest turbulence.

IMPLICATIONS – WHAT THIS MEANS TO YOU

The greatest industrial giants emerged during times of upheaval and turbulence. Entrepreneurs such as Rockefeller, Carnegie and J.P. Morgan came out of the shift from an agrarian to an industrial society. Companies like Hewlett-Packard, Apple Computer and Microsoft rose out of the shift to an electronic society.

During times of turbulence, many of the traditional paradigms that govern business are shattered. Consequently, companies and whole markets are seeking new solutions to the problems brought about by the forces of change.

It is important for sales managers to appreciate how creative thinking and decision making can greatly enhance their success during turbulent times. Rather than bemoan the loss of business due to a recession, sales managers should seek new opportunities brought about by market conditions. One thing is certain: companies are not going back to the business models of the 1990s. Instead, they are seeking new ways to enhance productivity and profitability; therein lies the opportunity for any sales manager. Sales managers should further note that in times of turbulence, the ability to anticipate what is on the horizon dramatically increases their chances of success.

STRATEGIES, TIPS & TECHNIQUES TO APPLY

If sales managers wish to take advantage of turbulent markets, they must apply creative thinking that enhances their decision making and facilitates new ways of looking at their business. The resultant shift in thinking allows them to develop new solutions to address their unit's problems and pinpoint the opportunities that are available to them. This creative thinking process includes the following elements:

Understanding Personal Influences

All sales managers are influenced by their own perceptions of reality, which creates a bias that shapes their view of the future. Typically these perceptions are created from the personal and professional experiences of the sales manager. For example, military generals plan for future conflicts based upon their experiences in past wars. Leaders that emerged by the end of World War II—Eisenhower, Bradley, Patton—were colonels and majors when the war began. The conflict gave them the ability to shine as leaders.

This example underscores the importance of sales managers transforming themselves into leaders. Leaders are driven by their passionate view of the possibilities of the future as defined by their vision. Leaders learn to rid themselves of their personal biases. They look to what is possible and then work toward that goal. In this way their perceptions of the past do not influence their view of the future.

Once sales managers can understand what influences their personal perceptions, they can take them into account as they step outside of their personal box and anticipate the future.

Divergent Thinking

Sales managers must adopt a mindset allowing them to acknowledge and discover more than one right answer to any problem. Divergent or "what if" thinking allows sales managers to seek out possibilities and opportunities and take advantage of them. Additionally, polished divergent thinking skills allow sales managers to keep their personal biases and perceptions from eliminating any possibilities until they are fully explored.

Convergent Thinking

Once sales managers have examined all available possibilities they must employ convergent thinking in integrating data and prioritize available choices. Sales managers apply analysis skills to determine the economic feasibility of each choice and to gauge its impact on the business.

Mapping and Imaging

In mapping, sales managers draw pathways illustrating how the organization will get from the present to the future. These pathways represent the goals and objectives that lead the company toward attainment of the desired overall outcome.

Imaging is the ability to create visual representations with words, graphs, or models to effectively communicate the future direction and vision of the company. This technique gives the sales manager the capacity to effectively communicate his or her vision for the company and the opportunities that present themselves in a manner readily understood by colleagues, salespeople and customers.

POINTS TO PONDER — SOMETHING TO THINK ABOUT

1. Do you perceive the current times as a period of opportunity or survival?
2. What prevents you from seeing the opportunities that may be present for your business?

TRAINING ACTIVITY — APPLICATION & ACTION PLAN

1. On a sheet of paper, list all of the perceptions you have about your company, products, industry and customers.
2. Next to each item, identify what has created that perception in your mind.
3. Determine whether each perception is accurate and realistic.
4. Identify those perceptions that may result in faulty thinking or misgivings regarding the future.

8

Factors Affecting Paradigm Thinking

Every company works under a paradigm, or written or unwritten set of rules and regulations delineating the boundaries of acceptable behavior in which one must operate in order to be successful. Such paradigms might be dictated by company policies or by an entire industry.

IMPLICATIONS – WHAT THIS MEANS TO YOU

Paradigms can be broken or shifted during times of turmoil and turbulence. Old partnerships and alliances are shattered as companies seek to streamline their operations. Entrenched vendors are uprooted as businesses seek more efficient and profitable solutions to their problems.

It is important for sales managers to realize that the complexion of business can change rapidly. The fact that customers routinely restructure their businesses carries both negative and positive implications for any company. Longtime established accounts may change their buying habits and open their doors to other suppliers, while other customers who were once uninterested open up to new ideas and solutions. Thus in many markets, the deck of cards is being shuffled; therein lies the opportunity for the sales manager who recognizes the dynamics of change as an ally.

STRATEGIES, TIPS & TECHNIQUES TO APPLY

Markets and customers are changing. This means that suppliers must also change to meet the new demands placed upon them. Undoubtedly, the companies most resistant to change will find themselves losing both customers and market share to more agile competitors.

Following is a list of traditional boundaries that govern most companies and their management. While not exhaustive, it does represent an excellent starting point for sales managers wishing to adapt their businesses to the forces of change. Sales managers must step outside of their normal frame of reference and question each of these boundaries and the rationale behind them. An examination (ideally conducted as a brainstorming session including all members of the management team) should question the validity of each and consider possible alternatives.

Management Theory

The management theory is the prevailing theory that governs the company. It is essentially the manner in which a company conducts its business. As the cornerstone of many businesses, it is seldom changed, yet may produce the best outcomes if modified to meet the changing demands of the marketplace.

Principles

Most businesses have a set of unwritten principles that all salespeople follow, which are normally established by past sales managers and have become the prevailing policy of the company. Problems arise if these principles have been codified over time and not reviewed for their effectiveness, efficiency and relevance to the market.

Focus

It is not unusual for a company to focus on internal issues such as productivity, return on investment and efficiency rather than on the needs of the customer. While these internal factors are important to the success of any company, sacrificing customer needs can be problematic. The focus should be carefully reviewed.

Standards

Standards are closely aligned with the company's focus. If the company is internally focused on production and procedures, then the standards will reflect this emphasis. Similarly, for the customer-focused company, emphasis is placed on customer-oriented standards that key in on value and overall satisfaction.

Assumptions

Every business unit builds their working model upon assumptions regarding the business environment, market behavior and customer behavior. Attention is required here because many of the assumptions being made about business environments have changed and continue to change. A failure to reexamine the assumptions upon which the business is operating can result in faulty models, inaccurate decisions and dire consequences.

Conventional Wisdom

Conventional wisdom embodies the combined perceptions of management regarding the company's business and market. It normally reflects the past successes and failures of the company and can bias management's thinking about the future while impacting the assumptions that are made. Conventional wisdom is also communicated throughout the company and typically shared by all salespeople.

During turbulent times where dramatic changes are occurring, it is important for management to examine the conventional wisdom that governs their behavior, as it is often not relevant or realistic.

Mindset

The mindset of the company reflects all of the aforementioned factors as well as management's thinking. The corporate mindset is communicated through all salespeople to customers, vendors and suppliers. In one specific instance a company communicated the fact that all customer problems were caused by "idiot operators" rather than a failure on its own part. This resulted in a number of customer and legal problems for the company.

Values

Company values and ethics have taken on increased importance in light of past events concerning Enron, Arthur Andersen and WorldCom. It is important that sales managers reevaluate their company's values to ensure they reflect the demands of their customers.

Traditions

Many longstanding company practices evolve into traditions, which can then reflect a thinking that communicates, "We've always done it this way." Traditions should be carefully examined, with those that inhibit change or don't make sense in the current business environment eliminated.

POINTS TO PONDER – SOMETHING TO THINK ABOUT

1. Do you think it is valuable to challenge the boundaries that define your business? Why or why not?
2. Are you reluctant to "rock the boat" in your company? Why or why not?

TRAINING ACTIVITY – APPLICATION & ACTION PLAN

1. Examine the list of boundaries that can be challenged in your business. Include other boundaries that should be examined by management.
2. Identify the boundaries that you feel need to be changed.
3. Identify alternatives to the current boundaries that you are challenging.
    - Management Theory
    - Principles
    - Focus

- Standards
- Assumptions
- Conventional Wisdom
- Mindset
- Values
- Traditions

About the Author

Timothy F. Bednarz, Ph.D. is CEO of the American Management Development Group, Inc. For over 20 years he has researched, designed and authored hundreds of learning and development programs used by Fortune 1000 companies.

He is also the author of *Great! What Makes Leaders Great. What They Did, How They Did It and What You Can Learn from It* (2011).

Speaking Availability

Timothy F. Bednarz, Ph.D. is available for speaking engagements for your next meeting or association event. He can be contacted at 800-654-4935 or by e-mail at timothy.bednarz@majorium.com.

Bulk Sales

Bulk sales of this book or any other titles available from Majorium Business Press. Inquiries can be directed to sales@majorium.com, or by phone at 800-6654-4935.

Quick Order Form

Fax orders: 715-342-1118. Send this form.

Telephone orders: Call 800-654-4935 toll-free. Have your credit card ready.

Email orders: sales@majorium.com

Postal orders: Majorium Business Press, 2025 Main Street, Stevens Point, WI 54481, USA.

Please send the following books:

____

____

____

____

Please send more FREE information on:

❑Catalog ❑Speaking/Seminars ❑Mailing Lists ❑Consulting

Name: ____

Address: ____

City: ________________________ State: _____ Zip: _________

Telephone: ____

Email address: _____________________________________

Sales tax: Please add 5.5% for products shipped to Wisconsin addresses.

Shipping by air:

United States: $4.00 for first book and $2.00 for each additional product.

International: $9.00 for first book; $5.00 for each additional product (estimate).

Made in United States
Cleveland, OH
05 November 2026

47664320R00030